# Contents

# The reason that Artist make a this book published

Jinsoo Youn (Artist / Writer)

This year marks the third year since I began writing about the progress of <Hidden Memories>, which I have been researching since entering graduate school. Regarding my works, which have been presented to the public through various exhibitions, I wanted the audience to easily understand the background of the creation of the works and the ideas contained in each work.

My research process, which will continue in the future, will be presented to the public on a regular basis through various methods. It could be published as a book, or it could be done through collaboration with instrumentalists.

Like the book's title, "After Hidden Memories," it comprehensively contains a series of works and performances starting from the production of the first work, "Hidden Memories," which began three years ago. What is most important is that the artist's philosophy is included in the works introduced in this book, which will help you understand the feelings conveyed to the audience for each work.

I recommend that viewers of my work take their time and change positions while viewing my work. This is because the intangible and invisible concepts of time and space are incorporated into my work. As you live in the universe with continuous space and time, you will realize that the forms that were not clear in your memory are not disappearing, but are hidden and are being newly created.

*Cette année marque la troisième année depuis que j'ai commencé à écrire sur les progrès de <Hidden Memories>, sur lequel je fais des recherches depuis mon entrée aux études supérieures. Concernant mes œuvres, qui ont été présentées au public à travers diverses expositions, je souhaitais que le public comprenne facilement le contexte de création des œuvres et les idées contenues dans chaque œuvre.*

*Mon processus de recherche, qui se poursuivra dans le futur, sera présenté régulièrement au public à travers diverses méthodes. Cela pourrait être publié sous forme de livre, ou cela pourrait être réalisé en collaboration avec des instrumentistes.*

*Tout comme le titre du livre, « After Hidden Memories », il contient de manière exhaustive une série d'œuvres et de performances commençant par la production de la première œuvre, « Hidden Memories», qui a débuté il y a trois ans. Le plus important est que la philosophie de l'artiste soit incluse dans les œuvres présentées dans ce livre, ce qui vous aidera à comprendre les sentiments transmis au public pour chaque œuvre.*

*Je recommande aux spectateurs de mon travail de prendre leur temps et de changer de position touten visionnant mon travail. En effet, les concepts intangibles et invisibles de temps et d'espace sont incorporés dans mon travail. En vivant dans un univers avec un espace et un temps continus, vous vous rendrez compte que les formes qui n'étaient pas claires dans votre mémoire ne disparaissent pas, mais sont cachées et sont de nouveau créées.*

# A background for selecting the Artist of the Year Award.

Seok Youn Yoo (National Culture Newspaper)

Artist Jinsoo Youn was selected as the Artist of the Year by the National Culture Newspaper. The following reasons can be cited in the background for selecting such award winners. In other words, over the past six years, he has consistently made various attempts to develop his work, and in addition to these artworks, he has attempted collaborations that connect his music performances with art exhibitions, demonstrating his original and broad new concept. This is because we are pioneering the field of art.

he also organizes and runs several art organizations and plans art exhibitions every year through continuous communication with his artists. These activities greatly contribute to introducing performing arts, a genre of Korean art and music, to the public through various social media platforms, and because of his significant contribution to the art field of our company, he was selected as the winner of the Artist of the Year Award.

Artist Jinsoo Youn has published a book containing his writings, which he painstakingly wrote based on the art works he has worked on over the past three years, along with photos of the art work <Hidden Memories>. Above all, it's very interested in the works he has exhibited in Italy and New York over the past six months, and we are looking forward to his various domestic and international exhibition activities this year as well. he has written in two languages, English and French in order to introduce his works at various art exhibitions held in France and the UK this year, and to ensure that the visitors can understand the background of his works.

*L'artiste Jinsoo Youn a été sélectionné comme artiste de l'année par le journal People. Les raisons suivantes peuvent être invoquées pour justifier la sélection de ces lauréats. En d'autres termes, aucours des six dernières années, il a constamment fait diverses tentatives pour développer son travailet, en plus de ces œuvres d'art, il a tenté des collaborations reliant ses performances musicales à des expositions d'art, démontrant ainsi son nouveau concept original et large. C'est parce que nous sommes pionniers dans le domaine de l'art.*

*il organise et dirige également plusieurs organisations artistiques et planifie des expositions d'art chaque année grâce à une communication continue avec ses artistes. Ces activités contribuent grandement à faire connaître au public les arts du spectacle, un genre d'art et de musique coréens, à travers diverses plateformes de médias sociaux, et en raison de sa contribution significative au domaine artistique de notre compagnie, il a été sélectionné comme lauréat du prix Artiste de le prix de l'année*

*L'artiste Jinsoo Youn a publié un livre contenant ses écrits, qu'il a minutieusement écrits à partir des œuvres d'art sur lesquelles il a travaillé au cours des trois dernières années, ainsi que des photos de l'œuvre d'art <Hidden Memories>. Surtout, il est très intéressé par les œuvres qu'il a exposées en Italie et à New York au cours des six derniers mois, et nous attendons avec impatience ses diverses activités d'exposition nationales et internationales cette année également. il a écrit en deux langues, l'anglais et le français, afin de présenter ses œuvres lors de diverses expositions d'art organisées en France et au Royaume-Uni cette année, et de s'assurer que les visiteurs puissent comprendre le contexte de ses œuvres.*

# About 'After Hidden Memories'

Bong Wook Lee (PhD. Art Criticism)

## Art is the act of revealing what is hidden

Jinsoo Youn sublimates his memories and experiences into art. In this way, he wants to reveal aspects of his overlapping memories. He uses lines and planes to create space and explore new dimensions. And he expresses something beyond memory through color and form. He opens up new visual dimensions through lines and planes. Entering through the open door, we can see the artist's process of exploring his inner self. The emotions and imagination that exist within the artist are created in this new space. We will be able to encounter various interpretations and experienes that he has constantly and diligently unfolded.

In the early work of <Hidden Memories> which was produced starting in 2021 and released the following year, the artist shows repeating the process of paint flowing down. One of the charms of a work of art is that a work of art is created through a combination of coincidence and clear intention. Artists often plan and express their works intentionally, but these accidental elements give new vitality to the work and make us more immersed in the uniqueness of the work.

In 2023, his work will develop further and change. He begins by attaching paper with adhesive material (from below, it referred to as 'glue paper') on the canvas and painting it with the desired color. And when the paint dries, the glue is removed, reapplied, and colored, creating a work of art through countless repetitions. The artist visually creates a new space through the effects of repeated layers of paper and acrylic paint to unravel the traces of the past, memories of the present, and future possibilities, creating a visual space that attempts to reinterpret the past, present, and future.

Since 2020, I have looked for common elements in the works that artist Jinsoo Youn has attemped, and became interested in the background that led to the creation of the current works. In other words, the artist cut out or tore off the paper by hand, attached newspaper or magazines to the canvas using a mixture of glue and various adhesive materials on the back, and then applied paint on it. Through another work, he devoted himself to expressing the traces that appear as he applies materials that stick well to the canvas, then attaches a series of tools to them and then removes them. The reason for this is that he was relatively more interested than other artists in the disappearance or appearance of traces as time passes and changes.

As the brush passes over an uneven surface, a boundary surface is created, and the artist did not pass by it but rather tried to lift it to the surface. Additionally, the foot print created through the process of burying and tearing off a part that shows strong viscosity would have been a good experiment for the artist. Based on the background knowledge and behavioral experience gained through the past three years of work, I think it is very natural that recent works incorporate the repetitive act of attaching adhesive paper to the canvas, letting paint pass over it, and then remoing it.

The journey of creating three-dimensional forms through his repetitive artistic actions can be said to be the core of creation in his works. He accumulated each experience and various memories he went through, and the present and the unseen future came together to form a single work of art. This creates a new perspective on life according to the way countless times and spaces are created, changed, and completed. The changes in forms revealed through this repetition send us silent messages and share meaningful emotions. Through this process, the meaning of the work will deepen through encounters with those who appreciate it.

The form he created is before us as a three-dimensional representational image of countless colors and traces of paper wrapped in layers. This reflects his desire to go beyond simple visual expression of the intention of art and explore the interaction between the inner world of humans and the external world. These numerous repetitions represent the world of memories experienced by the artist as a tool to express his emotions, thoughts, and aesthetic sense, and through this process, the work plays an important role in leading to a world beyond memories.

## Gaps create new things

Through the process of creating his works using glue paper and deconstructing traditional metods, we can get a glimpse of the artist's creativity and experimental desire. The various colors used in the work play an important role in visually conveying the artist's emotions and experiences. These colors communicate with the artist's inner world on the canvas, creating a space where dreams and reality come together, and at the same time expressing his emotions.

Glue paper, an important material for artist Jinsoo Youn, becomes a new work of art by repeating the process of attaching it to the canvas and applying paint several times. The sticky adhesive of layered paint and glue created during this process forms a new layer in the canvas expression, adding to the uniqueness of the work as a result that exceeds expectations. In particular, in the artist's expermental work using glue paper, it can be seen that a new three-dimensional image is created due to the unintended glue in the process of attaching and removing glue paper on the canvas. The artist's creative attempts and free artistic challenges expand the boundaries of art beyond its conventions and stimulate our imagination with new art forms and techniques.

The layer formed in this way resembles the 'thought of the gap' mentioned by Deleuze. For Deleuze, 'gap' is a place where new forms and ideas beyond traditional forms and norms are born. Artists expand the boundaries of art and discover new ways of expression through Deleuze's gap. It is in that gap that artistic innovation and experimental challenges are allowed. Deleuze's gap is an artistic space that accommodates diversity and complexity, and is a place to express the diverse perspectives, experiences, and stories of artists and create multi-layered and polysemous works.

Artist Jinsoo Youn creates a new layer through the process of attaching glue to the canvas and applying paint, and opens up new artistic possibilities through accidental effects expressed in the shape or texture of this layer. We discover new dimensions in the complexity expressed in this layer. The effect created as the paint flows and dries leaves traces on the surface of the object, forming a layer of time, and a special 'gap' is created in the work through the interaction between glue and paint.

This gap allows us to have artistic experiences. The layer formed through overlapping glue and paint also creates a new visual space. The gap in space shows the artist's deep understanding of himself and his emotional experiences, while at the same time going beyond simple visual elements, it shows the artist's recollections of his childhood and the traces he left behind in past spaces. The stories shown in the gaps between time and space become a new chapter where we recall our own past, evoke the journey expected in the future, and begin a new story about life.

Through the exhibition, the artist is unfolding the depth of color, form, and the potential of materals discovered in the process of creating works using glue. It will be an important time for writers to promote creative freedom and originality.

# 숨겨진 기억(Hidden Memories On The Letters)의 배경 및 의미

윤진수 (홍익대학교 미술대학원 미술학 석사)

2023년도에 시작된 내 최근 작품 <숨겨진 기억 (Hidden Memories On The Letters)> 를 작업하게 된 배경에 대해서 이렇게 적고 싶다. 이는 내가 어릴 적 살던 곳의 오래 전 일련의 목격한 경험을 기반으로 하게 된다. 내 기억 속의 일들이 생각났으며, 이를 내 최근 작품에 반영하게 되었다.

1980년대 내가 살던 곳은 한옥집이었으며, 장독대가 옥상과 같은 곳에 있었고 계단으로 그 곳을 올라갈 수 있는 곳으로 아파트 1층 높이 정도였다고 본다. 옛날 집들의 구조는 특별했던 것 같다.

어느 날 집 벽에 붙었던 포스터 종이가 전 날 내린 비로 인하여 물에 젖었고 종이가 쭈글쭈글한 상태로 붙어 있었던 것이다. 그리고 일부분은 내린 비와 바람에 의해 뜯겨나갔던 것이다. 그리고 비로 인하여 붓 같은 것으로 적어놓았던 글자 부분은 검게 번져서 무엇인지 읽을 수 없는 상태로 변해 있었다.

학교를 갔다 오는 사이에 날씨가 화창해지면서 해가 비춰 있었고 나는 한창 밖에서 놀다가 다시 집에 오는 길에 그 담벽을 보게 된 것이다. 작업하시는 분들이 그 벽에 새로운 포스터를 붙였는 데 이전에 비로 인하여 뜯겨져 있던 곳에 포스터 종이는 모서리 부분에 테이프 같이 부착을 위한 도구로 붙여져 고정되어 있었다. 만약 비가 다시 내리면 작업자들이 다시 와서 똑같은 일을 반복 하고 있었던 것 같다.

이렇게 포스터를 부착한 후에 바람이나 햇빛으로 인하여 어떠한 변형이 되어서 그 것을 제거를 하고 그 후에 새로운 것을 다시 부착하기 위해서 진행되었던 일련의 반복적인 과정들을 나는 내 작업에 적용하기 시작하게 된 것이다. 외형이 손상 된 무언가를 교체하기 위해서 뜯어내고 다시 붙이는 과정에서 나는 특별한 특징을 발견하게 된 것이다.

그것은 항상 그러한 기억의 상태나 변화가 반복적으로 나타난다는 것이며, 자아가 인지하는 그 순간을 기점으로 시간이 지나면서 이전에 있었던 상태보다 추가되거나 제거된 후, 변형을 통해 자연스럽게 이미지의 상태는 이전 모습을 유지하지 못했던 것이다.

그 동안 내 작품에서 기억이라는 대상으로만 한정하여 나는 과거와 현재, 그리고 미래의 시간의 연속적인 과정에서 꿈과 현실에서 기억 속에 존재하는 모호하게 혼재된 상태나 감정의 변화를 색과 형태를 통해 표현해 왔다. 그런데 기억 속 이미지(잔상)이 변화가 되고 새로운 상태로 바뀌는 것이 오히려 기억을 잘 이해하는 것이 아닌가 싶었다.

집 벽에 포스터에 적혀 있던 그 무언가가 기억에서 글자나 이미지의 형태와 같은 것을 나타내고 있고 어떤 외부 조건에 의해서 이전과 달리 시간이 지나면서 변형이 생기는 것에 중점을 두고 작업에 반영하게 된 것이 바로 Hidden Memories On The Letters 인 것이다.

문자의 형태가 변형되는 것을 나는 '왜곡'이라는 단어를 사용하게 되었으며, 그러한 왜곡이 일어나기 전의 상태는 우리들이 과거에 학습이라는 과정을 통해 인지하고 있던 것이다.

그러나 자연적이거나 인공적이거나 외부의 달라진 조건들로 인하여 그 학습 되어있던 기억 속에서의 무엇인가가 변형되어서 시간이 지난 후나 꿈과 현실을 오고 가는 과정에서 새롭게 창조된 것을 다시 인지하게 된다는 것이 바로 내 작품에서 표현하고자 하는 핵심내용일 것이다.

기억이 왜곡 되었으나, 시간이 흘러서 다시 새로운 상태를 자아는 받아들일 수밖에 없으며, 그 왜곡 되어가는 과정에서 자아가 인지할 때 감정의 상태가 결국 색채로 표현되는 것이다.

무엇보다 중요한 것은 내 기억 속의 형태의 왜곡은 꿈과 현실세계의 이동, 시간과 공간의 변화를 통해서 끊임없이 재창조 되어가는 과정이라는 것이다. 그것이 Hidden Memories On The Letters가 제작된 배경이다.

수많은 선이나 면은 이러한 반복적 행위를 하는 과정에서 자연스럽게 나타나는 시간과 공간의 변화를 우주 속으로 확장하게 된 함수를 나타낸 것이다. 그것은 기억 속에서의 에너지처럼 표현되기도 하며, 때로는 신경세포나 뉴런처럼 보이기도 한다.

시간이 흐르면서 기억을 하려는 자아의 애착과 노력은 점차 커져만 간다. 즉, 과거의 보다 오랜 시간으로 나의 기억을 돌려 놓고자 하는 어느 한 시점으로 사건을 이동시키기 위해서 결국 뇌의 기억을 온통 과거 사건에 집중시키게 된다. 그런데 보다 오랜 기억은 그 이후 시간에 발생 된 일련의 기억들로 인해서 숨겨진 것처럼 보이는 것이다.

만약 기억하고자 하는 과거 시간과 뇌 기능의 에너지를 생각해 본다면, 내가 태어난 시점으로 돌려놓는데 필요한 에너지는 아마도 어마 어마할 것이다. 불과 십분 전에 일어난 일을 기억하기 위해서는 작은 노력이 필요하지만, 한달 전에 일어난 일을 기억해 내기 위해서는 보다 몇 배로 많은 노력이 필요하기 때문이다. 그만큼 집중력도 동원되어야 할 것이다. 주변이 시끄러운 공간에 내가 있다면, 집중력도 분산되면서 어제의 일 조차 기억할 수 없는 것과 같은 이치이다.

기억은 인간의 고유 영역은 아니다. 뇌의 기능에는 신체의 동작에 명령을 주는 역할과 별도로 감각 기관을 통해 접수 된 일련의 사건들을 기억 저장소에 보관하고 유지해 준다. 그렇기 때문에 컴퓨터의 메모리의 역할을 하면서 주기적인 데이터 보관 및 유지를 위한 에너지의 공급이 필요하다.

과거의 일들을 기억하고자 하는 노력이 바로 에너지이며, 이러한 에너지는 내 주변의 외부 환경적 요인을 통해 그것은 만들어 진다. 그것은 자연 그 자체일 수도 있으며, 변화를 통한 외부 요인이 될 수도 있다. 즉, 우주 속의 에너지와 함께 시간과 공간적인 영향을 통해 변화되고 있는 바로 나의 기억이다. 신비로운 우주에는 다양한 에너지(Energy)가 존재하며 시간과 공간을 구성하는데 이용된다.

우주에 존재하는 행성들이 생성되기 전 한차례의 큰 폭발이 존재하였다고 말하는 빅뱅이론(Big Bang)처럼 어쩌면 이러한 큰 폭발이 일어나기 전에 한 점에 에너지 모두가 응축되어 있었을지도 모른다. (현재 나는 하나님의 창조섭리로 우주만물이 형성되었다는 것을 믿으며 살고 있다. 성경에도 창세기 1장을 보게 되면, 우주에 속한 것들의 창조 과정에 대해서 자세히 설명 되어있다.)

나는 대학에서 전자공학을 전공하면서 오랜 기간을 과학이론에 빠져서 살아왔다. 누구보다 우주에 관심이 많았고, 창조에 대한 부분이 연구 영역이었던 것이다. 이러한 일련의 관심과 경험들이 내 작품에 반영 된 것이다. 기억의 행동 역시 우주의 창조과정과 비슷하다고 생각하게 된 것이다. 즉, 우주가 조물주의 힘으로 낮과 밤이라는 시간을 보내면서 우주가 형성된 것처럼 작은 입자들이 창조되고 서로가 자연적으로 흩어지고 또한 유기적으로 모인 후, 새롭게 탄생하고 생성되는 과정의 반복이라고 생각한다.

어느 날 어떤 이유에서인지 아무리 노력해도 기억나지 않는 일련의 사건들이 갑자기 떠오르는 경우를 경험해 본 적이 있을 것이다. 기억은 작은 형태로 분해되어 사라지는 것이 아니라 어디론가 흩어졌다가 모여서 합쳐지고 주변 에너지의 흐름에 따라 생성된다. 이는 나타나지 않았을 뿐 어딘가 숨겨져 있던 것이며, 새롭게 재창조 되기 전의 상태로 나는 작품 속에 담은 것이다.

그것이 작품<Hidden Memories On The Letters>에서 기억을 우주 개념으로 확장하게 된 이유이다. 기억은 숨겨질 뿐 소멸되는 것이 아니다. 오히려 재창조 하기 위해서 잠시 흩어지는 과정에 있는 것이다. 기억이 신비로운 이유는 바로 어떻게 창조될지 알 수 없기 때문이다.

내 작품에서는 단순히 인간의 기억을 정적인 형태로 표현하는 것만으로는 절대 부족하다고 생각했고, <Hidden Memories On The Letters>라는 작품의 느낌은 최대한 역동적인 느낌을 관객에게 전달하고 있다고 생각한다. 우주 대폭발의 순간을 포착한 느낌은 물론, 호수에서 물고기가 헤엄치는 모습을 보기 위해 물 속을 들여다보는 순간, 햇빛이 쏟아지는 하늘을 올려다보는 장면도 작품을 통해 느낄 수 있다. 나의 작품을 통해서 바람에 날리는 대나무 숲을 볼 수 있을 것이다.

이런 의미에서 인간의 기억 시스템만큼 역동적인 메커니즘은 없을 것이다.

에너지는 눈에 보일 수 있지만 보이지 않는 경우가 많다. 고등학교 과학시간에 배우는 다양한 에너지 중 운동에너지, 위치에너지, 중력에너지는 일상생활에서 자연스럽게 경험할 수 있지만, 눈으로 볼 수 있거나 귀로 들을 수 있는 에너지는 아니다. 그래서 빛을 통해 시각적으로 느껴 볼 수 있도록 자전거를 예로 들어

설명하곤 했었다. 즉, 자전거의 페달을 밟으면 전면을 밝게 비춰주는 전구에 전기신호가 전달되어 불이 켜지는 것이다.

우리가 살고 있는 이 광활한 우주에는 따로 설명하지 않는 이상 개념으로만 이해해야 할 에너지들이 많다. 나는 <Hidden Memories On The Letters>라는 작품에서 이 광활한 우주 속에 존재하는 에너지의 개념을 담아내려고 노력해왔다.

꿈과 현실 사이에서 잔상처럼 남는 어렴풋이 기억되는 이미지들은 일련의 사건의 단편이나 문자적 형태도, 내가 경험하는 특정 시간에 국한된 것도 아닌, 상대적으로 발생하는 연속적인 시공간 변화 속에서 나타난다고 나는 생각하기 시작했다. 아마도 그것은 광활한 우주의 대형 시스템의 구조인 시간과 공간의 연속성과 상대성이 인간의 기억 속에도 존재한다는 이해일 것이다.

우리들은 광할한 우주 속에 살아 숨쉬는 자연과 함께한다. 자연은 항상 우리와 같은 모습을 유지하고 있는 것 같지만, 끊임없이 변화되고 소멸되었다가 새로운 종류로 만들어지고 있다.

나의 작품을 통해 살아 숨 쉬는 자연과 비유하는 경우가 있다. 그것은 일종의 캔버스에 사용되어진 다양한 색채의 레이어와 그로 느껴지게 되는 밀도감이 주는 이유 때문일 것이다.

길을 걷다가 길가에 보이는 나무와 나뭇잎 사이로 햇빛이 들어오는 그 느낌을 정말 좋아한다.

작년에 지나갈 때 보았던 모습과 올해 본 모습은 비슷하게 느껴지지만, 사계절이라는 시간을 지나고 추위와 더위를 같은 장소에서 견뎠을 것이다.

내 작품을 보는 관객에게 시간을 느끼게 하고 싶었으며, 오랜 시간이 작품안에 숨어있음을 전해주고 싶었다. 그런 배경이 두개 혹은 세개의 연작 그림이 만들도록 한 것이다.

# After Hidden Memories

## Après les souvenirs cachés

# Biography

I was born in Suwon in 1975, and currently live in Seoul. I started learning art in a special class in high school and chose electronic engineering as my major at Hanyang University, so I only pursued art as a hobby.

In 2018, I started making art again in earnest and won several awards at art contests. Of course, In the process, I held three solo exhibitions, and the exhibition experiences gave me the opportunity to dream of entering graduate school, so I will officially enroll in Hongik University's Graduate School of Fine Arts in 2020.

During graduate school, I learned a variety of art history, and through my interest in abstract art, I began researching <Trace of Time> and <Human Memory>. In 2022, an invitation exhibition was held based on a recommendation from a gallery in Seoul, and in 2023, solo exhibitions were held at art museums in Seoul and Gyeonggi-do. The work in the graduate art exhibition was <Hidden Memories>.

It expresses afterimages of memories and emotional states that appear as the experiences of the real world and the unconscious state or virtual world experiences that modern people can experience in repeated life environments are mixed in memory.

The title of this exhibition is "Hidden Memories On The Letters" a new series of "Hidden Memories" and was opened to external visitors for the first time in Milan, the site of the first overseas exhibition this year.

When we come across a symbol that appears vaguely rather than clearly, we realize that it is somehow different from the shape in our memory that we knew through learning in the past, so we can express the various emotions that appear at that time, and various "It was realized through a combination of colors and working with numerous repetitive layers."

On Preparing for An Exhibition in Milano…

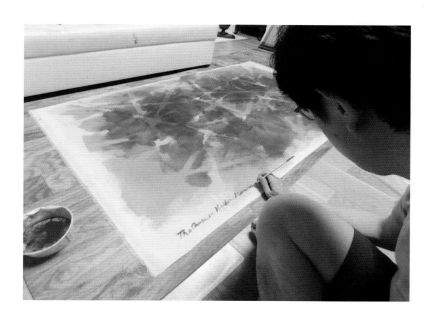

# Expressing the world of dreams and reality that exists in my memories

The motivation for creating the work began with an indistinct and vaguely remembered experence. The work was created based on vague afterimages in memories that were seen in a dream but appeared vaguely when one woke up and returned to reality.

*La motivation pour créer cette œuvre a commencé par une expérience indistincte et vaguement rappelée. L'œuvre a été créée sur la base de vagues images rémanentes dans des souvenirs vus dans un rêve mais qui sont apparues vaguement au réveil et au retour à la réalité.*

**Seong Nam Art Center Korea, Jan. 2023**

One day, I fell into a deep sleep and experienced a reality-like fantasy in my dream. I had such a dream about three times during the recovery period from my caught by COVID-19, and as I began to abstractly put the vague shapes I saw in those dreams into paintings, a series of works were created. From Early of Mar 2022 - Before finishing Hongik Graduate School), I started studying the relationship of between a dream and real-world in human memory in depth. I think this is the motive for creating. The 14 representative works were selected from the series that were created for 12 months with various emotions and forms obtained through this inspiration, and the photos and descriptions of the works were translated into three languages and included in the exhibition catlog.

*Un jour, je suis tombé dans un sommeil profond et j'ai vécu un fantasme semblable à la réalité dans mon rêve. J'ai fait un tel rêve environ trois fois pendant la période de récupération après avoir été attrapé par le COVID-19, et alors que je commençais à mettre de manière abstraite les formes vagues que je voyais dans ces rêves dans des peintures, une série d'œuvres ont été créées. Depuis début mars 2022 - avant de terminer la Hongik Graduate School), j'ai commencé à étudier en profondeur la relation entre un rêve et le monde réel dans la mémoire humaine. Je pense que c'est le motif de la création. Les 14 œuvres représentatives ont été sélectionnées parmi les séries créées pendant 12 mois avec diverses émotions et formes obtenues grâce à cette inspiration, et les photos et descriptions des œuvres ont été traduites en trois langues et incluses dans le catalogue de l'exp sition.*

**Hidden Memories, 162.2 X 130.3cm, Acrylic and Ink on canvas, 2022**

My artistic work focuses on a state encountered in human memory. it expresses afterimages of memories and emotional states that appear as the experiences of the real world and the unconscious state or virtual world experiences that modern people can experience in repeated life environments are mixed in memory. Through continued research, the work evolved and developed, becoming more abstract with distorted images of literal shapes that appear in memory in situations where dreams and the real world intersect.

In general, when we come across a symbol that appears vaguely rather than clearly, we realize that it is somehow different from the shape in our memory that we knew through learning in the past. so we can express the various emotions that appear at that time, It was realized through a combination of colors and working with numerous repetitive layers. There are so many emotions and history in Human Memory and changed from their born. in that process which time passing it, the shape could be different with the original one in memory. I continuously add the layer of various colors repeatedly on the shape at the same time while it's drawing line.

*Mon travail artistique se concentre sur un état rencontré dans la mémoire humaine. il exprime des images rémanentes de souvenirs et d'états émotionnels qui apparaissent lorsque les expériences du monde réel et l'état inconscient ou les expériences du monde virtuel que les gens modernes peuvent expérimenter dans des environnements de vie répétés sont mélangés dans la mémoire. Grâce à des recherches continues, l'œuvre a évolué et s'est développée, devenant plus abstraite avec des images déformées de formes littérales qui apparaissent dans la mémoire dans des situations où les rêves et le monde réel se croisent.*

*En général, lorsque nous rencontrons un symbole qui apparaît vaguement plutôt que clairement, nous réalisons qu'il est en quelque sorte différent de la forme dans notre mémoire que nous connaissions grâce à nos apprentissages passés. afin que nous puissions exprimer les différentes émotions qui apparaissent à cette époque, cela a été réalisé grâce à une combinaison de couleurs et en travaillant avec de nombreuses couches répétitives. Il y a tellement d'émotions et d'histoire dans la mémoire humaine et qui ont changé depuis leur naissance. dans ce processus, au fil du temps, la forme pourrait être différente de celle d'origine en mémoire. J'ajoute continuellement le calque de différentes couleurs à plusieurs reprises sur la forme en même temps que la ligne est tracée.*

**Key Gallery, Milano Italy, Oct. 2023**

During the production process of the work , I reinterpreted the creative composition and principles of the image showing a certain letter shape expressed from my perspective. In other words, it symbolizes the process of being repeatedly recreated in a new third form that will be encountered in memory by dismantling and decomposing in the function of time and space. Eventually the title of exhibition was hold on this year is "Hidden Memories On The Letters" which was updated from a connected series of "Hidden Memories" and it was opened to external visitors for the first time in Milan (Italy) the site of the first overseas exhibition on October 2023.

*Au cours du processus de production de l'œuvre, j'ai réinterprété la composition créative et les principes de l'image montrant une certaine forme de lettre exprimée de mon point de vue. En d'autres termes, il symbolise le processus de recréation répétée sous une nouvelle troisième forme qui sera rencontrée dans la mémoire en se démantelant et en se décomposant en fonction du temps et de l'espace. Finalement, le titre de l'exposition de cette année est "Souvenirs cachés sur les lettres", mis à jour à partir d'une série connectée de "Souvenirs cachés", et elle a été ouverte aux visiteurs externes pour la première fois à Milan (Italie), sur le site de l'exposition. première exposition à l'étranger en octobre 2023.*

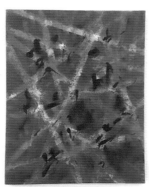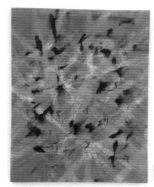

**Hidden Memories On The Letters (No.23-III-40, 47, 44), 40.9 x 31.8cm, Acrylic and Ink on canvas, 2023**

# Understanding space and time through the repetitive act of drawing lines

Hidden Memories In my early work, I devised a way of working. It was to express different worlds. In other words, as the canvas is repeatedly painted using the working brush, many lines are drawn repeatedly in diagonal and straight directions, creating a sense of space inside and outside. The purpose was to consciously create another world (dream) separate from the world outside the painting (reality) while looking at the work.

*Souvenirs cachés Dans mes premiers travaux, j'ai imaginé une façon de travailler. C'était pour exprimer des mondes différents. En d'autres termes, lorsque la toile est peinte à plusieurs reprises à l'aide du pinceau, de nombreuses lignes sont tracées à plusieurs reprises dans des directions diagonales et droites, créant une impression d'espace à l'intérieur et à l'extérieur. Le but était de créer consciemment un autre monde (le rêve) séparé du monde extérieur au tableau (la réalité) tout en regardant l'œuvre.*

**While painting <Hidden Memories> in the art studio , 2022**

Modern people are trapped in time and space where only concepts exist and are not visible to the eye. It is an isolated place where you go back and forth between the unconsciousness of a dream and the real world, and even if you see different images in your memory, they are always blocked by the same time pattern. The accumulation of lines means that simple repetitive actions that started in the past are accumulating over time, and this temporal continuity proves the connection between dreams and the real world. The lines and surfaces drawn further inward were created at a time before the lines and surfaces drawn more externally.

*Les gens modernes sont piégés dans le temps et dans l'espace où seuls des concepts existent et ne sont pas visibles à l'œil nu. C'est un lieu isolé où vous faites des allers-retours entre l'inconscient d'un rêve et le monde réel, et même si vous voyez des images différentes dans votre mémoire, elles sont toujours bloquées par le même schéma temporel. L'accumulation de lignes signifie que des actions simples et répétitives commencées dans le passé s'accumulent au fil du temps, et cette continuité temporelle prouve le lien entre les rêves et le monde réel.*

*Les lignes et les surfaces dessinées plus vers l'intérieur ont été créées à une époque antérieure aux lignes et surfaces dessinées plus vers l'extérieur. En d'autres termes, dans le processus par lequel le moi se réveille d'un rêve et revient à la réalité, le temps du rêve est plus passé que le temps du monde réel.*

**Jiguchon Gallery Korea, Feb. 2023**

As I experience a series of ambiguous shapes through dreams, I begin to see unusual patterns in my work. I began to express afterimages of images in my memory. These forms are drawn to transcend the division of territories, that is, the separate worlds (dream and reality) that cannot coexist. This is because afterimages of memories remain ambiguous in dreams and reality.

*Alors que je fais l'expérience d'une série de formes ambiguës à travers mes rêves, je commence à voir des motifs inhabituels dans mon travail. J'ai commencé à exprimer des images rémanentes d'images dans ma mémoire. Ces formes sont dessinées pour transcender la division des territoires, c'est-à-dire les mondes séparés (rêve et réalité) qui ne peuvent coexister. En effet, les images rémanentes des souvenirs restent ambiguës dans les rêves et dans la réalité.*

**Hidden Memories (No.22-II-06 09, 08), 162.2 X 130.3cm, Acrylic and Ink on canvas, 2022**

This is because the experiences or emotions seen in a dream are stored for a short time in a place called memory, not somewhere else, even after waking up from the dream and returning to reality. This is because experiences of events or actions that occurred in the past still have an influence even after returning from reality to the unconscious state of a dream.

*En effet, les expériences ou les émotions vues dans un rêve sont stockées pendant une courte période dans un endroit appelé mémoire, et non ailleurs, même après le réveil du rêve et le retour à la réalité. En effet, les expériences d'événements ou d'actions survenues dans le passé ont toujours une influence même après le retour de la réalité à l'état inconscient d'un rêve.*

**Hidden Memories, 162.2 X 130.3cm, Acrylic and Ink on canvas, 2022**

Characters and shapes stored in the storage of memories were expressed with the effect of appearing or disappearing. These shapes and letters have been visually recognized repeatedly since childhood, and what remained in my memory for a long time was expressed through my work. The forms or expressions of emotions depicted in the work may be new events that appeared in a dream, or they may be actual events that the ego experienced in the past. The images seen while dreaming may be events that have never occurred in reality, but even in an unconscious state, events that occurred in the past appear mixed together.

*Les caractères et les formes stockés dans le stockage des souvenirs étaient exprimés avec pour effet d'apparaître ou de disparaître. Ces formes et lettres ont été visuellement reconnues à plusieurs reprises depuis l'enfance, et ce qui est resté longtemps dans ma mémoire s'est exprimé à travers mon travail. Les formes ou expressions d'émotions représentées dans l'œuvre peuvent être de nouveaux événements apparus dans un rêve, ou bien des événements réels que l'ego a vécus dans le passé. Les images vues en rêvant peuvent être des événements qui ne se sont jamais produits dans la réalité, mais même dans un état inconscient, les événements survenus dans le passé semblent mélangés.*

# Discovering literal forms lost in memory

I would like to write this about the background of my latest work, <Hidden Memories On The Letters>, which began in 2023. This is based on a series of experiences I witnessed a long time ago in the place where I lived as a child. Things from my memory came to mind, and I reflected them in my recent work. The place I lived in the 1980s was a Hanok house, and the crock pot was on the same roof. You could go up the stairs and it was about the height of the first floor of an apartment building. The structure of old houses seems to have been special.

One day, the poster paper that was attached to the wall of the house was soaked with water due to the rain the previous day, and the paper was stuck in a wrinkled state. And some parts were torn off by the rain and wind. And due to the rain, the letters that had been written with a brush or something were blurred black and became unreadable. While I was coming home from school, the weather got brighter and the sun was shining, and I played outside and on my way home again, I saw that wall. The workers had put up a new poster on the wall, and where it had previously been torn off due to rain, the poster paper was attached to the corner with a tape-like attachment tool. If it rained again, the workers would likely come back and do the same thing again.

*Je voudrais écrire ceci sur le contexte de mon dernier travail, <Hidden Memories On The Letters>, qui a commencé en 2023. Il est basé sur une série d'expériences dont j'ai été témoin il y a longtemps dans l'endroit où je vivais quand j'étais enfant. . Des choses de ma mémoire me sont venues à l'esprit et je les ai reflétées dans mon travail récent. L'endroit où je vivais dans les années 1980 était une maison Hanok et la mijoteuse était sur le même toit. On pouvait monter les escaliers et c'était à peu près la hauteur du premier étage d'un immeuble. La structure des maisons anciennes semble avoir été particulière.*

*Un jour, le papier pour affiche qui était fixé au mur de la maison était trempé d'eau à cause de la pluie de la veille, et le papier était coincé et froissé. Et certaines parties ont été arrachées par la pluie et le vent. Et à cause de la pluie, les lettres qui avaient été écrites avec un pinceau ou quelque chose comme ça étaient floues en noir et devenaient illisibles. Alors que je rentrais de l'école, le temps s'est éclairci et le soleil brillait, et j'ai joué dehors et en rentrant chez moi, j'ai vu ce mur. Les ouvriers avaient accroché une nouvelle affiche sur le mur et, là où elle avait été arrachée à cause de la pluie, le papier postal a été fixé au coin à l'aide d'un outil de fixation semblable à du ruban adhésif. S'il pleuvait encore, les ouvriers reviendraient probablement et feraient la même chose.*

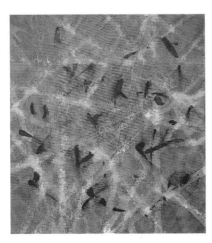 

**Hidden Memories On The Letters (No.23-III-59, 60), 53.0 X 45.5cm, Acrylic and Ink on canvas, 2023**

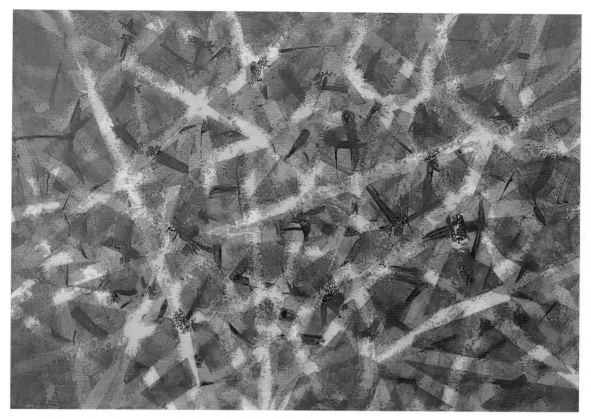

**Hidden Memories On The Letters (No.23-III-66), 53.0 X 72.7cm, Acrylic and Ink on canvas, 2023**

After attaching a poster like this, it was deformed in some way by wind or sunlight, so I removed it and then reattached a new one. I began to apply the series of repetitive processes that followed to my work. In the process of tearing apart and putting back together to replace something whose appearance had been damaged, I discovered a special characteristic.

This means that such memory states or changes always appear repeatedly, and as time goes by starting from the moment the ego recognizes, additions or removals from the previous state are made, and through transformation, the state of the image naturally returns to its previous appearance. It was not possible to maintain it.

*Après avoir fixé un poteau comme celui-ci, il a été déformé d'une manière ou d'une autre par le vent ou la lumière du soleil, je l'ai donc retiré, puis j'en ai refixé un nouveau. J'ai commencé à appliquer à mon travail la série de processus répétitifs qui ont suivi. En démontant et en remontant pour remplacer quelque chose dont l'apparence avait été endommagée, j'ai découvert une caractéristique particulière.*

*Cela signifie que de tels états ou changements de mémoire apparaissent toujours de manière répétée et, au fil du temps, à partir du moment où l'ego le reconnaît, des ajouts ou des suppressions par rapport à l'état précédent sont effectués et, par transformation, l'état de l'image revient naturellement à son apparence précédente. . Il n'était pas possible de le maintenir.*

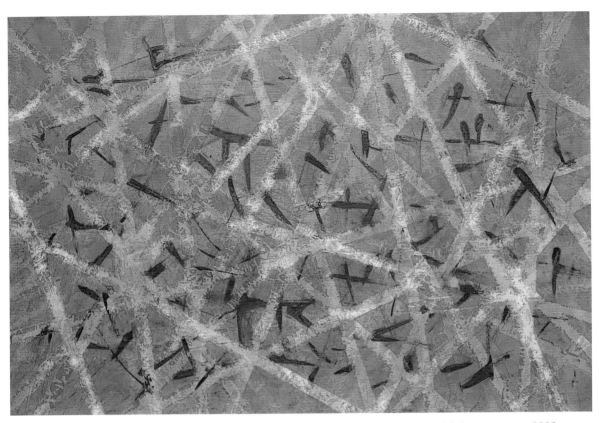

Hidden Memories On The Letters (No.23-III-67), 65.1 X 90.9cm, Acrylic and Ink on canvas, 2023

So far, in my work, I have limited myself to the subject of memory and have expressed through color and form the ambiguously mixed states and changes in emotions that exist in memories in dreams and reality in a continuous process of past, present, and future time. However, I thought that changing the image (afterimage) in the memory and changing it into a new state would be a better way to understand the memory.

Something written on a poster on the wall of the house represents something like a letter or image in memory, and the fact that changes occur over time due to external conditions, unlike before, was reflected in the work, which is what Hidden Memories On The Letters.

*Jusqu'à présent, dans mon travail, je me suis limité au sujet de la mémoire et j'ai exprimé à travers la couleur et la forme les états et les changements d'émotions ambiguës qui existent dans les souvenirs des rêves et de la réalité dans un processus continu de passé, présent et futur. temps. . Cependant, je pensais que changer l'image (image rémanente) dans la mémoire et la changer dans un nouvelétat serait une meilleure façon de comprendre la mémoire.*

*Quelque chose d'écrit sur une affiche accrochée au mur de la maison représente quelque chose comme une lettre ou une image en mémoire, et le fait que des changements se produisent au fil du temps en raison de conditions extérieures, contrairement à avant, se reflète dans l'œuvre, ce qui estce que "Hidden Memories On Les lettres."*

# Memory image constantly recreated through change

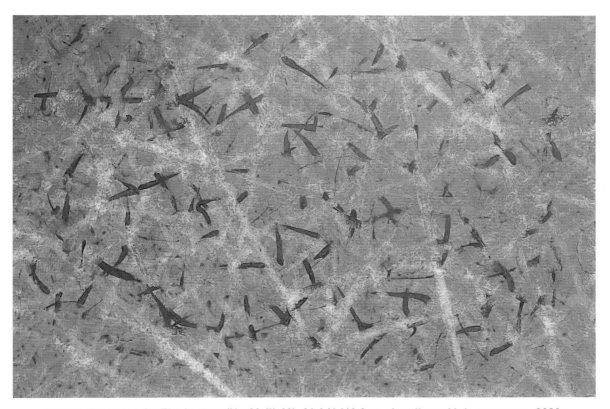

**Hidden Memories On The Letters (No.23-III-69), 80.3 X 116.8cm, Acrylic and Ink on canvas, 2023**

I came to use the word 'distortion' to describe the shape of a letter being transformed, and the state before such distortion occurred was something we recognized in the past through a process called learning.

However, in my work, due to changing natural, artificial, or external conditions, something in the learned memory becomes variable, and after time passes or in the process of going back and forth between dreams and reality, something newly created is recognized again. This may be the core content you want to express.

*J'en suis venu à utiliser le mot « distorsion » pour décrire la forme d'une lettre en cours de transformation, et l'état avant qu'une telle distorsion ne se produise était quelque chose que nous reconnaissions dans le passé grâce à un processus appelé apprentissage.*

*Cependant, dans mon travail, en raison de l'évolution des conditions naturelles, artificielles ou externes, quelque chose dans la mémoire apprise devient variable, et après le temps ou dans le processus d'aller-retour entre les rêves et la réalité, quelque chose de nouvellement créé est à nouveau reconnu. Cela peut être le contenu principal que vous souhaitez exprimer*

**Hidden Memories On The Letters (No.24-III-71), 91.0 X 116.8cm, Acrylic and Ink on canvas, 2024**

The memory is distorted, but as time passes, the ego has no choice but to accept the new state, and when the ego recognizes it in the process of distortion, the emotional state is ultimately expressed in color.. The distorted shape of the letter does not disappear from memory over time, but is recreated.

What is most important is that the distortion of the form in my memory is a process of constant recreation through the movement between dreams and the real world and changes in time and space. That is the background behind the creation of Hidden Memories On The Letters.

*La mémoire est déformée, mais à mesure que le temps passe, l'ego n'a d'autre choix que d'accepter le nouvel état, et lorsque l'ego le reconnaît dans le processus de distorsion, l'état émotionnel s'exprime finalement en couleur. La forme déformée de la lettre ne disparaît pas de la mémoire avec le temps, mais est recréée.*

*Ce qui est le plus important, c'est que la distorsion de la forme dans ma mémoire est un processus de recréation constante à travers le mouvement entre les rêves et le monde réel et les changements dans le temps et dans l'espace. C'est le contexte derrière la création de Hidden Memories On The Letters*

# Memories expanded into the universe through space-time energy

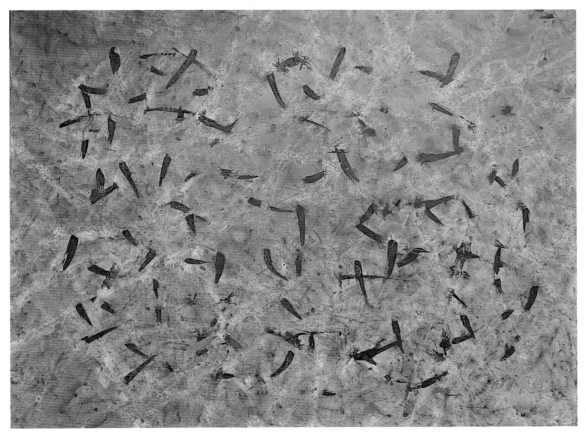

**Hidden Memories On The Letters (No.24-III-72), 91.0 X 116.8cm, Acrylic and Ink on canvas, 2024**

The numerous lines and planes represent the functions that extend the changes in time and space that occur naturally in the process of these repetitive actions into the universe. It is expressed like energy in memory, and sometimes looks like nerve cells or neurons

As time passes, the ego's attachment and effort to remember gradually increases. In other words, in order to move the event to a certain point in time where I want to return my memory to a longer period of time in the past, I end up focusing my brain's memory entirely on past events. However, older memories seem to be hidden due to a series of memories that occurred at a later time.

*Les nombreuses lignes et plans représentent les fonctions qui prolongent les changements dans le temps et l'espace qui se produisent naturellement au cours du processus de ces actions répétitives dans l'univers. Elle s'exprime comme l'énergie dans la mémoire, et ressemble parfois à des cellules nerveuses ou à des neurones.*

*À mesure que le temps passe, l'attachement de l'ego et ses efforts de mémorisation augmentent progressivement. En d'autres termes, afin de déplacer l'événement à un certain moment où je souhaite ramener ma mémoire à une période plus longue du passé, je finis par concentrer entièrement la mémoire de mon cerveau sur les événements passés. Cependant, les souvenirs plus anciens semblent être cachés en raison d'une série de souvenirs survenus plus tard.*

**Hidden Memories On The Letters (No.24-III-73), 91.0 X 116.8cm, Acrylic and Ink on canvas, 2024**

If you think about the energy of past time and brain function to remember, the energy required to return to the time when I was born would probably be enormous. It takes a small amount of effort to remember something that happened just ten minutes ago, but it takes several times more effort to remember something that happened a month ago. You will need to mobilize your concentration as well as your muscles. If you are in a noisy space, your concentration will be scattered and you will not even be able to remember yesterday's events. Memory is not a unique domain of humans. Apart from giving commands to the body's movements, the brain's function is to store and maintain a series of events received through sense organs in memory storage. Therefore, while serving as the compu er's memory, it is necessary to supply energy for periodic data storage and maintenance.

*Si vous pensez à l'énergie du temps passé et aux fonctions cérébrales dont il faut se souvenir, l'éne gie nécessaire pour revenir à l'époque de ma naissance serait probablement énorme. Il faut un petit effort pour se souvenir de quelque chose qui s'est produit il y a à peine dix minutes, mais il faut plusieurs fois plus d'efforts pour se souvenir de quelque chose qui s'est produit il y a un mois. Vous devrez mobiliser votre concentration ainsi que vos muscles. Si vous êtes dans un espace bruyant, votre concentration sera dispersée et vous ne pourrez même pas vous souvenir des événements de la veille. La mémoire n'est pas un domaine unique aux humains. En plus de commander les mouvements du corps, la fonction du cerveau est de stocker et de maintenir dans la mémoire une série d'événements reçus par les organes des sens. Par conséquent, tout en servant de mémoire à l'ord nateur, il est nécessaire de fournir de l'énergie pour le stockage et la maintenance périodiques des données.*

**Hidden Memories On The Letters (No.24-III-74), 91.0 X 116.8cm, Acrylic and Ink on canvas, 2024**

The effort to remember past events is energy, and this energy is created through external environmental factors around me. It may be nature itself, or it may be an external factor through change. In other words, it is my memory that is changing through temporal and spatial influences along with the energy in the universe. Various energies exist in the mysterious universe and are used to construct time and space.

Like the Big Bang theory, which states that there was a large explosion before the planets in the universe were created, perhaps all of the energy was condensed in one point before such a large explosion occurred. (Currently, I live believing that all things in the universe were formed through God's creation providence. If you look at Chapter 1 of Genesis in the Bible, the creation process of things in the universe is explained in detail.)

*L'effort pour se souvenir des événements passés est une énergie, et cette énergie est créée par des facteurs environnementaux externes qui m'entourent. Cela peut être la nature elle-même, ou cela peut être un facteur externe dû au changement. En d'autres termes, c'est ma mémoire qui change sous l'effet des influences temporelles et spatiales ainsi que de l'énergie de l'univers. Diverses énergies existent dans l'univers mystérieux et sont utilisées pour construire le temps et l'espace.*

*Comme la théorie du Big Bang, qui affirme qu'il y a eu une grande explosion avant la création des planètes de l'univers, peut-être que toute l'énergie a été condensée en un point avant qu'une telle explosion ne se produise. (Actuellement, je vis en croyant que toutes choses dans l'univers ont été formées grâce à la providence créatrice de Dieu. Si vous regardez le chapitre 1 de la Genèse dans la Bible, le processus de création des choses dans l'univers est expliqué en détail.)*

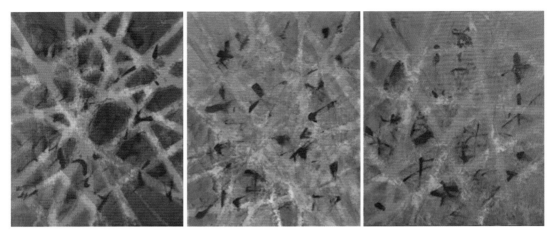

**Hidden Memories On The Letters (No.23-III-48, 50, 58), 45.5 X 37.9cm, Acrylic and Ink on canvas, 2023**

While majoring in electronic engineering in college, I have been immersed in the field of science for a long time. I was more interested in the universe than anyone else, and creation was my area of research. These series of interests and experiences are reflected in my work. The act of memory was also thought to be similar to the creation process of the universe. In other words, I think it is a repetition of the process of small particles being created, naturally dispersing and gathering organically, and then being born and created again, just as the universe was formed through the time of day and night by the power of the Creator.

You may have experienced a case where one day, a series of events that you could not remember no matter how hard you tried suddenly came to mind due to some reason. Memories do not break down into small forms and disappear, but are scattered somewhere and then gathered, merged, and created through the flow of surrounding energy. It just didn't appear, it was hidden somewhere, and I captured it in my work in its state before it was newly recreated. That is why in the work <Hidden Memories On The Letters>, memory was expanded to the concept of the universe. Memories are only hidden, not extinguished. Rather, it is in the process of dispersing for a while in order to be re created. The reason memories are mysterious is because we cannot know how they are created.

*Alors que je me spécialisais en génie électronique au collège, je suis immergé dans le domaine des sciences depuis longtemps. Je m'intéressais plus que quiconque à l'univers et la création était mon domaine de recherche. Cette série d'intérêts et d'expériences se reflète dans mon travail. On pensait également que l'acte de mémoire était similaire au processus de création de l'univers. En d'autres termes, je pense qu'il s'agit d'une répétition du processus de création de petites particules, se dispe sant naturellement et se rassemblant de manière organique, puis nées et recréées, tout comme l'univers s'est formé au fil du jour et de la nuit par le pouvoir de l'énergie. le créateur.*

*Vous avez peut-être vécu un cas où un jour, une série d'événements dont vous ne vous souveniez pas, malgré tous vos efforts, vous sont soudainement venus à l'esprit pour une raison quelconque. Les souvenirs ne se décomposent pas en petites formes et ne disparaissent pas, mais sont dispersés quelque part puis rassemblés, fusionnés et créés grâce au flux d'énergie environnante. Il n'est tout simplement pas apparu, il était caché quelque part et je l'ai capturé dans mon travail dans son état avant qu'il ne soit recréé. C'est pourquoi, dans l'ouvrage <Hidden Memories On The Letters>, la mémoire a été élargie au concept d'univers. Les souvenirs sont seulement cachés, pas éteints. Au contraire, il est en train de se disperser pendant un certain temps afin d'être recréé. La raison pour laquelle les souvenirs sont mystérieux est que nous ne pouvons pas savoir comment ils sont créés.*

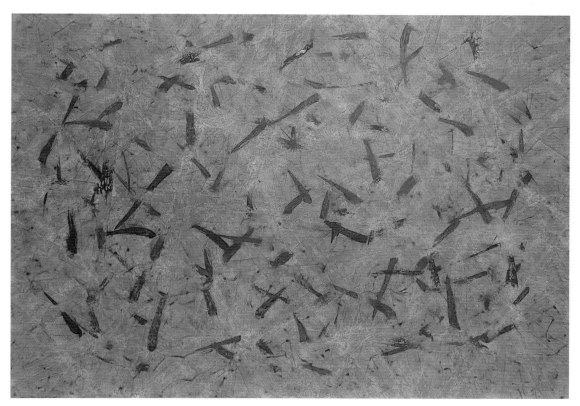

**Hidden Memories On The Letters (No.23-III-70), 65.1 X 90.9cm, Acrylic and Ink on canvas, 2023**

In my work, I thought that it was absolutely insufficient to simply express human memories in a static form, and as much as possible, the feeling of the work <Hidden Memories On The Letters> conveyed a dynamic feeling to the audience. I think I am doing it. In addition to the feeling of capturing the moment of the great explosion of the universe, you can also feel the moment of looking into the water to see fish swimming in the lake, or the scene of looking up at the sky with sunlight falling in the bamboo forest blowing in the wind. There may be no mechanism as dynamic as the human memory system.

*Dans mon travail, je pensais qu'il était absolument insuffisant d'exprimer simplement les souvenirs humains sous une forme statique, et autant que possible, le sentiment de l'œuvre <Hidden Memories On The Letters> transmettait un sentiment dynamique au public. Je pense que je le fais. En plus de la sensation de capturer le moment de la grande explosion de l'univers, vous pouvez également ressentir le moment de regarder dans l'eau pour voir des poissons nager dans le lac, ou la scène de regarder le ciel avec la lumière du soleil tombant dans le forêt de bambous soufflée par le vent. Il n'existe peut-être aucun mécanisme aussi dynamique que le système de mémoire humaine.*

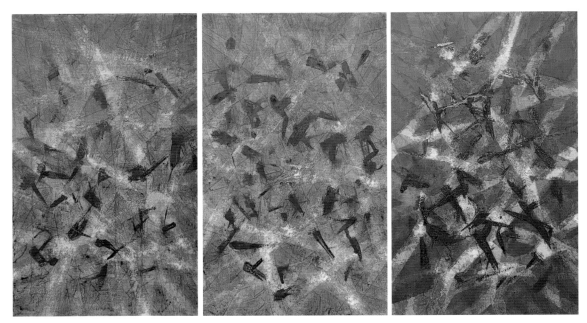

**Hidden Memories On The Letters (No.23-III-62, 64, 65), 45.5 X 27.3cm, Acrylic and Ink on canvas, 2023**

Energy can be visible, but it is often invisible. Among the various energies learned in high school science classes, kinetic energy, potential energy, and gravitational energy can be naturally experienced during our daily lives, but they are not energies that can be seen with the eyes or heard with the ears. So, I used to explain it using a bicycle as an example so that we could see it through light. In other words, when you step on the pedal of a bicycle, an electrical signal is transmitted to the light bulb that brightly illuminates the front, and the light turns on.

In this vast universe we live in, there are many energies that must be understood only as concepts unless explained through something else. I have tried to include the concept of energy in this vast universe in my work <Hidden Memories On The Letters>.

*L'énergie peut être visible, mais elle est souvent invisible. Parmi les différentes énergies apprises dans les cours de sciences au lycée, l'énergie cinétique, l'énergie potentielle et l'énergie gravitatio nelle peuvent être naturellement ressenties au cours de notre vie quotidienne, mais ce ne sont pas des énergies visibles avec les yeux ou entendues avec les oreilles. Alors, j'avais l'habitude de l'expl quer en utilisant un vélo comme exemple pour qu'on puisse le voir à travers la lumière. En d'autres termes, lorsque vous appuyez sur la pédale d'un vélo, un signal électrique est transmis à l'ampoule qui éclaire vivement l'avant et la lumière s'allume.*

*Dans ce vaste univers dans lequel nous vivons, il existe de nombreuses énergies qui doivent être comprises uniquement comme des concepts, à moins d'être expliquées par autre chose. J'ai essayé d'inclure le concept d'énergie dans ce vaste univers dans mon travail <Hidden Memories On The Letters>.*

**Goyang Eoulim Museum Korea, Nov. 2023**

The vaguely remembered images that remain like afterimages between dreams and reality are not fragments of a series of events, literal forms, or limited to the specific time I experience them, but appear in the continuous changes in time and space that occur relatively. I started thinking. Perhaps it is an understanding that the continuity and relativity of time and space, which are the structure of the large system of the vast universe, exist even in human memory.

*Les images vaguement rappelées qui restent comme des images rémanentes entre les rêves et la réalité ne sont pas des fragments d'une série d'événements, des formes littérales, ou limitées au moment précis où je les vis, mais apparaissent dans les changements continus dans le temps et dans l'espace qui se produisent de manière relative. J'ai commencé à réfléchir. Peut-être s'agit-il de co prendre que la continuité et la relativité du temps et de l'espace, qui constituent la structure du vaste système du vaste univers, existent même dans la mémoire humaine.*

# Memories created from feelings given by nature

## Winter

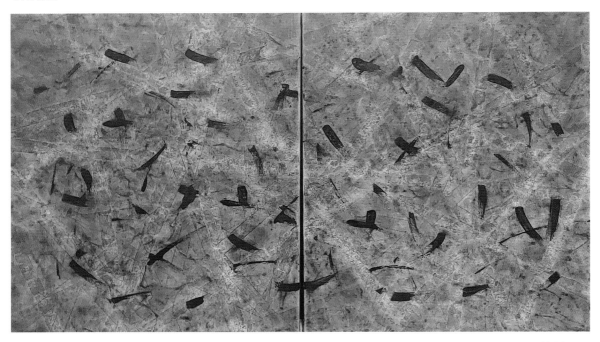

**Hidden Memories On The Letters (No.24-III-76, 77), 45.5 X 27.3cm, Acrylic and Ink on canvas, 2024**

We live together with nature, which lives and breathes in the vast universe. Nature seems to always remain the same as us, but it is constantly changing, disappearing, and creating new types. There are times when I compare my work to living, breathing nature. This may be due to the layers of various colors used on a kind of canvas and the density felt through them

I really like the feeling of sunlight coming through the trees and leaves along the road while walking. The sight I saw last year and the sight I saw this year feel similar, but they must have endured the cold and heat in the same place after four seasons.I wanted to make the audience watching my work feel the passage of time, and convey that a long time was hidden in the work. That background was what led to the creation of two or three series of paintings.

*Nous vivons avec la nature, qui vit et respire dans le vaste univers. La nature semble toujours rester la même que nous, mais elle change constamment, disparaît et crée de nouveaux types. Il y a des moments où je compare mon travail à la nature vivante et respirante. Cela peut être dû aux couches de différentes couleurs utilisées sur une sorte de toile et à la densité ressentie à travers elles. Dans ce vaste univers dans lequel nous vivons, il existe de nombreuses énergies qui doivent être comprises uniquement comme des concepts, à moins d'être expliquées par autre chose. J'ai essayé d'inclure le concept d'énergie dans ce vaste univers dans mon travail <Hidden Memories On The Letters>.*

*J'aime beaucoup la sensation du soleil qui traverse les arbres et les feuilles le long de la route en marchant. Le spectacle que j'ai vu l'année dernière et celui que j'ai vu cette année sont similaires, mais ils ont dû endurer le froid et la chaleur au même endroit après quatre saisons. Je voulais que le public qui regarde mon travail ressente le passage du temps et transmette que longtemps était caché dans l'œuvre. C'est ce contexte qui a conduit à la création de deux ou trois séries de peintures.*

## Autumn

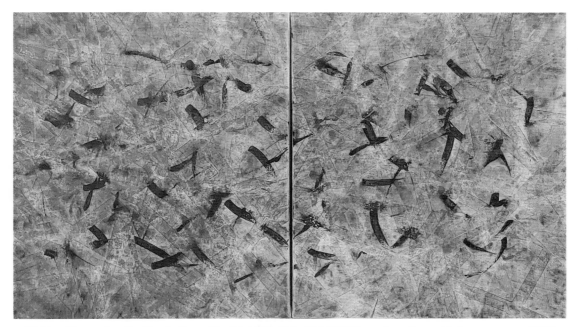

**Hidden Memories On The Letters (No.24-III-78, 79), 45.5 X 27.3cm, Acrylic and Ink on canvas, 2024**

## Spring & Summer

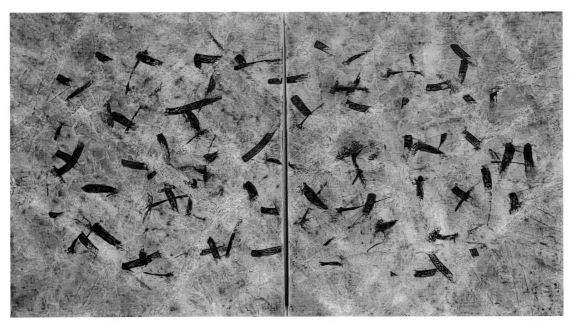

**Hidden Memories On The Letters (No.24-III-80, 81), 45.5 X 27.3cm, Acrylic and Ink on canvas, 2024**

# Hidden Memories on the Music

I was planning an exhibition of my newly created work in the winter of 2022 to make it more mea
ingful. For a long time, I have wanted to present a collaborative stage where music performance
and art exhibitions are held together. In order to create the work motivated by that, I started using
<Hidden Memories On The Music>, which was included in the exhibition poster, as a subtitle.

*Je prévoyais une exposition de mon travail nouvellement créé à l'hiver 2022 pour lui donner plus
de sens. Depuis longtemps, je souhaitais présenter une scène collaborative où se déroulent
ensemble performances musicales et expositions d'art. Afin de créer l'œuvre motivée par cela, j'ai
commencé à utiliser comme sous-titre <Hidden Memories On The Music>, qui était inclus dans
l'affiche de l'exposition.*

**Hidden Memories On The Music, Seongnam Art Center, Jan. 2023**

**Violinist Keunha Yer, Seongnam Art Center, Jan 26th 2023**

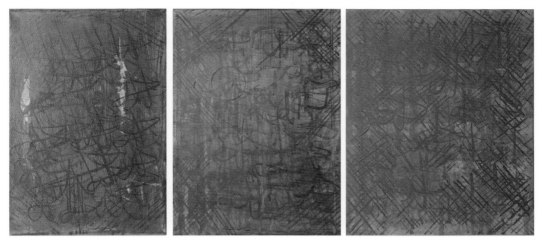

**Hidden Memories On The Music (No.23-III-19, 18, 17), Acrylic and Ink on canvas, 2023**

Hidden Memories On The Music (No.23-III-19, 18, 17), Acrylic and Ink on canvas, 2023 I began to find various materials that would remain in the long-lasting memories of musicians, and I began to draw them on canvas. How to read musical scales and the conductor's hand movements for beats were things that had to be learned in order to play music on a daily basis. When you repeatedly transfer these things to your memory through practice and actually perform them, the images and musical symbols in your memory that you practiced in advance come to mind. The works from this time were introduced to external audiences at a gallery in Korea.

*J'ai commencé à trouver divers matériaux qui resteraient dans la mémoire durable des musiciens et j'ai commencé à les dessiner sur toile. Comment lire les gammes musicales et les mouvements de la main du chef d'orchestre pour les rythmes étaient des choses qu'il fallait apprendre pour jouer de la musique au quotidien. Lorsque vous transférez ces choses à plusieurs reprises dans votre mémoire par la pratique et que vous les exécutez réellement, les images et les symboles musicaux dans votre mémoire que vous avez pratiqués à l'avance vous viennent à l'esprit. Les œuvres de cette époque ont été présentées au public extérieur dans une galerie*

**Ton Art Place Gallery Korea, Apr. 2023**

**Hidden Memories On The Music, KEPCO Art Center, May 25th 2024**

In May of this year, the second story of Hidden Memories On The Letters was delivered to the audience with a beautiful melody. At the end of January last year, a collaboration exhibition with a performance by a world-class violinist Keunha Yer was held, which received favorable reviews from many audiences for creating an innovative exhibition in connection with music. In this second story, I will play the piano myself and collaborate musically with violinist Professor Keunha Yer to guide the audience watching the work into their memories through different time and space, such as dreams and the real world.

*En mai de cette année, la deuxième histoire de Hidden Memories On The Letters a été livrée au public avec une belle mélodie. Fin janvier de l'année dernière, une exposition collaborative avec une performance d'un violoniste de classe mondiale a eu lieu, qui a reçu des critiques favorables de la part de nombreux publics pour la création d'une exposition innovante en lien avec la musique. Dans cette deuxième histoire, je jouerai moi-même du piano et collaborerai musicalement avec la viol niste professeur Keunha Yer pour guider le public qui regarde l'œuvre dans ses souvenirs à travers différents temps et espaces, tels que les rêves et le monde réel.*

# Youn Jin Soo (尹眞守)

b.1975 Suwon Korea
Hongik University Graduate School of Fine Arts Painting(M.F.A)
Hanyang University Electronics
Hongik University Graduate School Alumni International Exchange Chairperson
Hongwoo Painting Art Exhibition Chief Executive (2021 ~ )
Reve (Christian Painting Art Group) Executive (2023 ~ )

## Solo Exhibitions

*2024* Hidden Memories - After (KEPCO Art Center Gallery, Seoul) - *May.2024*
2023 Hidden Memories On The Letters (Key Gallery, Milano, Italy)
2023 Hidden Memories (Invitation Exhibition, TonArt Gallery, Seongnam)
2023 Hidden Memories (Jiguchon Gallery, Seongnam)
2023 Hidden Memories (Gyeomjae Jeongseon Art Museum, Seoul)
2023 Hidden Memories On The Music (Seongnam Art Center Gallery)
2022 Trace of Time (Invitation Exhibition, ARTEM Gallery, Seoul)
2020 Korean Beauty (Euljiro Atelier Gallery)
2019 Korean Beauty (Jongno Chohyung Gallery)
2019 Korean Beauty (Gangseo Cultural Center)

## Group Exhibitions

*2024* Hongwoo Painting Art Exhibition 4th 'Depth Of Emotions' - *Jul.2024*
2023 New York Times Square Art Show Promotive Artists(Plogix, New York)
2023 Hongwoo Painting Art Exhibition 3rd 'Sometimes Happy, Sometimes Sad'
2022 Hongik University Painting/Sculpture 'AROOM' (ARTEM)
2022 Hongwoo Painting Art Exhibition 2nd 'Return To Innocence'
2022 Hongik University Painting Exhibition (Chohyung Gallery)
2021 Hongwoo Painting Art Exhibition 1st 'Cheong Myung'
2021 Hongik University Painting Exhibition (Gosaek Newseum)

Art Fair

*2024* Paris Carrousel du LOUVRE ART Shopping 2024 (Paris) - *Apr.2024*
2024 Taipei Hotel Hyatt ART Fomosa 2024 (Taipei) - Jan. 2024
2023 Seoul International Art EXPO 2023 (Samsung dong COEX, Seoul)

## Awards

2024 11th Abstract International Prize - Honorable Mention Award (by TERVARNA)
2024 Artist Award of the Year (by National Culture Newspaper, Korea)
2021 Korea Art International Grand Exhibition (Western Painting Part)
2020 Kyeongin Great Arts Exhibition (Korean Painting Part)
2020 Korea Art International Grand Exhibition (Western Painting Part)
2019 Peace Foundation for Arts and Culture (Korean Painting Part)
2019 Korea Art International Grand Exhibition (Western Painting Part)
2019 Peace Arts Grand Exhibition (Korean Painting Part)
2018 Peace Foundation for Arts and Culture (Korean Painting Part)

# 2024 Art Prize

## International 11th Abstract International Prize (by TERVARNA)

### HONORABLE MENTION AWARD

*11th*

# ABSTRACT

International Juried Art Competition
February 2024

# WINNERS

**331 artists from 42 countries**
won in one of six prize categories
Winners will be prominently featured in multiple
media platforms.

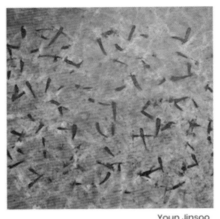

**Youn Jinsoo**
Hidden Memories On The Letters (No.24-Ⅲ-72) | Acrylic |
SOUTH KOREA

We're delighted to bring you the exciting news that you have won the HONORABLE MENTION AWARD in the "11th ABSTRACT" art competition along with other distinguished artists. If you have any questions about the exhibition or its procedural requirements, please feel free to ask. Again, congratulations on your well-deserved win, and we hope to highlight many more of your artistic contributions for our upcoming exhibitions.

*Nous sommes ravis de vous annoncer la nouvelle passionnante que vous avez remporté le PRIX HONORABLE MENTION dans le cadre du concours d'art "11ème ABSTRAIT" aux côtés d'autres artistes distingués. Si vous avez des questions sur l'exposition ou ses exigences procédurales, n'hésitez pas à les poser. Encore une fois, félicitations pour votre victoire bien méritée et nous espérons mettre en valeur de nombreuses autres contributions artistiques pour nos prochaines expositions.*

**[Feburary 7th 2024, Provided by Gallery Manager of TERAVARNA]**

# National 2024 Artist Award of the Year (by National Culture Newspaper, Korea)

The National Culture Newspaper recognized the contribution of artist Jinsoo Youn, who contributed to promoting and developing the company's image in the field of art and performance both domestically and internationally through creative creative activities, and selected him as the winner of the Artist of the Year Award.

Artist Jinsoo Youn graduated from Hongik University's Graduate School of Fine Arts with a Master's degree in Painting and is active as an artist both at home and abroad. In particular, his representative series, "Hidden Memories," was held in Milan, Italy on October 10 last year and received positive reviews from various overseas visitors. Additionally, on December 16, representative works of his latest series, <Hidden Memories On The Letters>, were introduced on a large screen in New York's Times Square, leaving a deep impression on many overseas visitors.

*Le journal People a reconnu la contribution de l'artiste Jinsoo Youn, qui a contribué à la promotion et au développement de l'image de l'entreprise dans le domaine de l'art et de la performance, tant au niveau national qu'international à travers des activités créatives, et l'a sélectionné comme lauréat du prix de l'artiste de l'année.*

*L'artiste Jinsoo Youn est diplômée de l'École supérieure des beaux-arts de l'Université Hongik avec une maîtrise en peinture et est active en tant qu'artiste tant dans son pays qu'à l'étranger. En particulier, sa série représentative, « Hidden Memories », s'est tenue à Milan, en Italie, le 10 octobre de l'année dernière et a reçu des critiques positives de la part de divers visiteurs étrangers. De plus, le 16 décembre, des œuvres représentatives de sa dernière série, <Hidden Memories On The Letters>, ont été présentées sur un grand écran à Times Square à New York, laissant une profonde impression sur de nombreux visiteurs étrangers.*

**[Feburary 3rd 2024, By National Culture Newspaper]**

Ricordi nascosti - Hidden Memories
Mostra personale di Youn Jin Soo
Key Gallery, via Pietro Borsieri 12 Milano
Dal 10 al 12 ottobre 2023
Opening martedì 10 ottobre ore 18.00

Youn Jin Soo artista sud coreano vincitore di numerosi premi e riconoscimenti, per la prima volta in mostra in Italia a Milano alla Key Gallery la sua intrigante ed evocativa serie di opere "Hidden Memories".

Le immagini esprimono i ricordi degli stati emotivi che appaiono mentre si mescolano alla memoria le esperienze del mondo reale e le esperienze dello stato inconscio o del mondo virtuale che le persone moderne possono sperimentare nella quotidianità.

"Ho cominciato a interessarmi ai ricordi latenti dei sogni e della realtà accumulati dal passato al presente, esprimendo le emozioni trovate tra le memorie nascoste nei meandri della mente come se le esperienze dei sogni e della realtà fossero impilate in strati con il trascorrere del tempo.
La serie di opere si espande ,studiata per più di un anno a partire dal 2020.
Le tracce sono rimaste sulla Terra insieme alla natura mentre l'ambiente cambia nel tempo e nello spazio. Alla fine, ho collegato queste tracce alle esperienze di vita e ho rappresentato il fenomeno che permane come immagine residua nei sogni e nella realtà".
Youn Jin Soo

**The Articles in the Milano Today (Newspaper), Oct 3rd 2023 (Registered by Key Gallery)**

# 2023 The Exhibition of the Screens in Times Square New York, USA

**Hidden Memories On The Letters, Times Square New York, Dec 15th 2023 (Provided by Plogix)**

**The Crowded people in Times Square New York, Dec 16th 2023 (Captured by EarthCam)**

# *Après les souvenirs cachés*

## 책 제작에 참여한 사람들 (production participant)

**지은이: 윤진수(Writer & Composer : Jinsoo Youn)**

홍익대학교 미술대학원 미술학 석사졸업(M.F.A)
한양대학교 전자공학 학사
홍우회화전 운영회장('21~ )
크리스챤 미술선교단체 '레브' 대표('23~ )

E-Mail : edwardyoon7@gmail.com
Blog : https://blog.naver.com/edwardyoon7
Instagram : @edwardyoon7

**연주자(바이올린 콜라보): 여근하 (Violinist : Keunha Yer)**

미국 Oikos University 박사 D.M.A, D.Min
독일 Weimar 국립음대 석사 및 최고연주자 과정I
독일 Weimar 국립음대 Orchester Akademie
한양대학교 음악대학 학사
미국 Oikos University 교수
여음 아트컴퍼니 대표

YouTube : https://youtube.com/@keunhayer
Instagram ID : @keunhayer

**미술 평론가: 이봉욱 (Art Criticism : Bongwook Lee)**

홍익대학교 일반대학원 예술학 박사졸업(Ph.D. Art Theory & Criticism)
프랑스 파리 13대학 커뮤니케이션학과 전시개념 전공 최고과정 수료
프랑스 파리 8대학 조형예술학 학사, 석사 졸업
아르떼(Arte) 문화예술콘텐츠연구소 소장
갤러리 아인(Gallery Eyn) 대표

E-Mail : eyn2411 @gmail.com
Instagram ID : @galleryeyn_arte

디자인 : 김지희**(Designer : Jihee Kim)**, Instagram ID : @jihuipig
프로필 사진 : 엄광헌**(Profile Photo : Kwangheon Eom)**, @rabbi_studio

# 숨겨진 기억 이후
## After Hidden Memories

발 행 인 | 마수희
발 행 처 | 도서출판 엘비즈      발 행 일 | 2024. 03. 08
주      소 | 서울특별시 금천구 가산디지털1로 128 에스티엑스브이타워 B1 119호(가산동)
등록번호 | 제2019호-000004호